MANNERS

Hello ~ English

Bonjour ~ French

你好 ~ Mandarin

Hola ~ Spanish

Hallo ~ German

Jambo or Huambo ~ Swahili

TABLE MANNERS

Saideh A. Brown

GS Publishing Group
New York City
June 2024

A special thank you to my business coach, Mr. Bill Davis of Team Nimbus.

Ms. Novelty, Sandra Mayo, thank you for believing in the HPX Method.

I love you Shoshanna.
You make everyone better.

Table Manners.

I have been a student my entire life; I have learned from many. If you read something in my book that sounds like something you may have heard elsewhere it is purely coincidental. The words in this book are my own.

Published and printed the United States

GS Publishing Group

ISBN-13: 978-0-9793642-8-0

Dedicated to my mom, Khadija Akmal;
who founded The Etiquette Academy in 1976.

Education gets you in the room.

Social Intelligence keeps you in the room.

Etiquette gets you invited back.

Table of Contents

In the quiet moments of introspection, I often find myself reflecting on my journey of self-growth. It's a journey marked not by grand achievements or external accolades, but by subtle shifts within—the gradual molding of character, the broadening of perspective, and the deepening of understanding.

Growing up, the expectation in my household was clear and uncompromising: I was not allowed to get a grade below an A. Period. This parental directive, while undoubtedly well-intentioned, cast a long shadow over my formative years and deeply influenced my approach to academics, career, relationships, and life. I never became the best hooper in high school because I was always afraid to "take the shot!" because I might miss. I settled into an unlikely marriage because I was afraid I'd cycle through relationships. And, I slowly became a recluse, out of fear of not showing up in the highest possible way. My loving and caring family had damaged me in the most incurable of ways. Initially, this emphasis on academic excellence fueled my ambition. Showing up prepared, well rested, belly full and with all hairs on my head in place gave me an edge towards academic excellence. By those standards alone I was ahead of so many others of my generation. By middle school my self-worth showed up in the most elitist of ways; by high school I was a full-blown snob.

I attended high school in New York City – not Brooklyn or the Bronx or Queens (no knock to them) but on the island of Manhattan. This 13-mile city, one of the most powerful cities in the world, ate its own. In 1986, at the start of our sophomore year, my friends and I began meeting for breakfast each day at a diner on 23rd Street and 8th Avenue, a five-minute walk from our school High School for the Humanities. We typically missed the first two periods as long as we made it into the building by mid-morning for home room headcount, we were counted present for the day.
We were living in the belly of the New Jack City crack era and met each morning to show off our fits. Rising corner boys from Brooklyn

and Harlem kept us laced. We wanted to see which one of us was rockin' the latest tan Gucci bag with the matching boots; or who was carrying the biggest MCM bag. Queen Bee for the day was reserved for whomever was wearing a custom fit from Dapper Dan.

By senior year, in 1989, our breakfast club expanded to include girls from other boroughs whose jewelry came from Tiffany's too; and whose bags were as expensive as ours, but we seemingly spoke a different language during breakfast. Our parents were investment bankers, titans of industry, professors, music industry executives, and magazine publishers whose social networks – and ultimately ours – were anchored within a protected network of society. The changing economic and social landscape blurred the socioeconomic lines, but we were all still friends. We shared the same core values, but once the school day ended, we went home to very different places in the city. The evolving nature of class and wealth grew too quickly for the elite social class in the city at the time. Macy's and New York City's luxury retailers didn't want our money no matter what part of the city we called home, they didn't want us in their presence. Young black kids with money and some sense represented a threat to their elitist norm.

Dapper Dan, born Daniel Day, started out selling furs in Harlem. With access to cash flowing freely among young people he scaled his business quickly by making his own garments using a self-taught fabrication method that closely matched the textiles of the luxury fashion houses. Unlike the stores on Fifth Avenue that shunned our money, his 24/7 boutique in Harlem welcomed the gangsters, rappers and drug dealers (and their girlfriends). Powered by Fendi's jealousy, intellectual property theft claims and haters in law enforcement, Dapper Dan's shop was raided in 1992. We were *his* customer base. And, even though they didn't want our money, they didn't want him to have it either; the deception by all sides was revealed in that raid.

In the years that followed our ghetto-fabulous ascent, aided by Dap's style and ingenuity among other things, America changed into something it never experienced before. A fast-rising underclass. In 2012, ad executive Steve Stoute released the book *The Tanning of America: How Hip-Hop Created a Culture That*

Rewrote the Rules of the New Economy; a 320-page opus on the redefined psychosocial colorways of America's elite. Society wanted to make America great again, so it criminalized our wealth. But they were too late; we already learned the silent language of cutlery.

Table Manners was written from the practical use of etiquette at my mom's insistence starting from five years old, when she started teaching etiquette. I didn't have the option to not sit properly at the table. Of the many gifts I received for my 9th birthday, few were as practical as a shiny-silver Cross™ pen and personalized stationery. From that moment on I wrote thank you notes for *everything*.
My mother, having grown up in challenging circumstances, instilled in me the importance of good etiquette, writing thank-you notes, and practicing good manners. For her, these were not just niceties but essential tools for easily navigating a world that often judges based on appearances and first impressions.

Through her guidance, I learned that good etiquette isn't about pretense or formality but about showing respect for others and appreciating the kindnesses extended to us.

Writing thank-you notes became a way to express genuine gratitude, and acknowledge the efforts of others in a small and inexpensive way. Her lessons have stayed with me, shaping not only how I interact with people but also how I navigate professional settings and build lasting relationships. Those lessons are a testament to her resilience and wisdom, passed down to me as invaluable tools for success.

Impeccable etiquette signals belonging and cultivates trust among peers and business partners. It opens doors to exclusive networks where knowledge and opportunities are shared discreetly. Manners, such as courteous behavior and proper dining etiquette, reflect upbringing and reinforce social standing. My mother craved that for me, and for herself. Good etiquette validated us. Teaching etiquette to our children instills values of respect, consideration, and cultural awareness in future generations. It's essential for maintaining business relationships and navigating complex family dynamics that can either support or undermine wealth preservation. Lack of etiquette hinders wealth creation by alienating potential investors, partners, or clients. Inheritance is more than assets; it's about passing down a legacy of social capital built on etiquette and manners. Etiquette and manners are not superficial customs but assets that contribute to the longevity and growth of generational wealth; fostering a legacy of respect and influence that extends beyond financial success. It's the connector of journeys and the manifestation by which self-discovery, and resilience are revealed.

Etiquette is the strategy and manners are the tactic. They are the invisible threads that weave through social and professional interactions, influencing opportunities, alliances, and reputation. It's how our bloodline is codified for years to come.

Blessings,

 Saideh

Spades

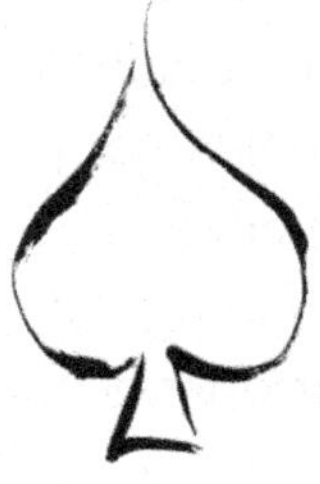

In the card game of Spades, there's a fascinating dynamic where all players can see the cards each person holds, yet the outcome of the game hinges on how those cards are strategically played—a concept akin to Sun Tzu's philosophy in "The Art of War."

Imagine you're sitting around a table with friends, each player is dealt a hand of cards. You lay your cards face-up on the table for all to see, creating a sense of transparency. Everyone knows what you have, and you know what they have in return. This open display might seem to level the playing field, but in reality, it introduces a deeper layer of strategy and psychology. While your opponents can see your cards, they can't dictate how you'll play them. They might anticipate your moves based on your visible hand, (ie: what they think they know about you) but your decisions—when to bid aggressively, when to strategically discard, or when to lead a particular suit—are entirely your own. Your goal is not just to have good cards, but to use them in a way that maximizes your chances of winning the most tricks, or possibly "set" your opponents. This dynamic mirrors Sun Tzu's insight: "All men can see the tactics whereby I conquer, but what none can see is the strategy out of which victory is evolved."

In Spades, as in war and life, it's not just about the cards you hold or the immediate moves you make, but the overarching strategy that guides your decisions throughout the game. Your strategy involves anticipating your opponents' moves, adapting to changing circumstances, and leveraging your hand's strengths to win.

While your opponents can see your cards, they can't play your hand for you. It's *your* strategic thinking, *your* ability to read the game, and *your* tactical decisions that ultimately determine whether you win or lose. It's a reminder that transparency in information doesn't equate to predictability in outcomes—there's always room for strategic maneuvering and surprises that can turn the tide in your favor.

Use etiquette as a strategic framework; and manners as a tactical tool to scale up, manage relationships and navigate cultural differences. In a globalized world, etiquette enables you to adapt seamlessly to different environments, showing sensitivity to customs and traditions while forging mutually beneficial relationships.

Etiquette disarms your opponents, nay-sayers and oppressors; and reimagines the historical landscape of your perpetual wins. It gets you a seat at the table; where grace, respect, and consideration are your trump cards for navigating every interaction with finesse and success.

You're Invited

Receiving an invitation is a moment that marks the beginning of an enriching social experience. It's an opportunity to make connections, shine and celebrate with class, and create lasting relationships.

The invitation is a gesture of kindness and consideration extended by the host. It shows that they value your presence and wish to share an occasion with you. It's a moment when someone has thought of you, crafted a guest list, and taken the time to formally invite you into their world, whether for a joyous celebration, event or an important gathering. Do not take an invitation for granted, everybody didn't receive one. The invitation, no matter the size of the event, has granted you access to a network that can make or break you. Value the host and plan your presence. Other guests may hold key positions in elite companies, industries, and philanthropic organizations; networking among these giants can provide access to opportunities, internships, mentorship programs, and financial advancement resources. Building genuine relationships among the other guests should extend beyond your immediate career goals. Savy guests can spot a charlatan a mile away. If you're not getting the invitations you'd like to receive, then it's time you up your game. Elite social circles encompass a spectrum of spaces, from high-society gatherings and clubs to industry-specific events and philanthropic galas. Each with its own codes of conduct, mandates, expectations, and pathways for entry. Know the rules of engagement before bullying or buying your way in. Check here first.

Your current network: Your current network is the most direct route to connecting up. Leverage existing connections, and ask for introductions from mutual contacts.

Private clubs. Clubs often host social events, member mixers, and recreational activities that can facilitate connections.

Industry associations: Join your industry associations or professional organizations.
Be visible at conferences and on committees.

Alumni networks. Alumni events and reunions provide a platform to reconnect with former classmates.

Cultural events. Attend art exhibits, the theater or other culture-rich experiences to socialize in sophisticated settings.

Luxury events. Attend car shows, yacht expos, fashion weeks, or auctions. These events attract lifestylists who appreciate fine living.

Taste new things. Cigars and a nice spirit are a great equalizer. Lounges and clubhouses provide a relaxed environment for networking and forging business relationships.

Dine out. Dine at upscale restaurants and eateries. Sit at the bar or communal tables to strike up conversations with other patrons.

Philanthropy. Get involved by volunteering for, donating to or serving on a board or committee for a reputable non-profit.

Taste New Things. Cigars and a nice spirit are a great equalizer. Lounges and clubhouses provide a relaxed environment for networking and forging new relationships.

Play Golf. Golf courses and clubhouses offer a setting where conversations can be enjoyed without force or haste.

Use concierge services. Utilizing a concierge service, either offered by a hotel, a private club or through a private relationship connects you to their network and their lifestyle.

Travel. Travel to luxury destinations and stay at high end resorts and hotels. Engage with fellow guests during spa treatments, private excursions, or cocktail hours.

Move! My mother told me, pointedly, to live in the least expensive house in the most expensive area I could afford. I grew up at 160 Bleecker Street in New York City's Greenwich Village area. First, in apartment 3K West, then in apartment 1A West. My mother, stepfather and me lived in a studio apartment. Right next to our building was one of the hottest jazz clubs in the city at the time – The Village Gate, owned by acclaimed jazz aficionado Art D'Lugoff. Uncle Art let me sneak behind the bar after school and pour a glass of soda if I promised to do all of my homework. Performers at The Gate, and their kids, always found their way into our apartment. Before long, we moved into a bigger apartment in the building – with two bedrooms and two bathrooms. No one cared that we once lived in a studio in the same building, the flex was *where* we lived, not how. Moving to a bigger apartment simply allowed our social network to grow. And with that came more money and more access.

Beyond superficial mingling, authenticity matters. While getting invited to VIP events may seem like a perk reserved for the privileged few, its significance extends far beyond the glitz and glamour. It represents a gateway to access, professional advancement, visibility, knowledge acquisition, and personal enrichment—mission critical components for success in today's interconnected and competitive world.

The next time you receive a coveted invitation, embrace it as a stepping stone towards new horizons and endless possibilities.

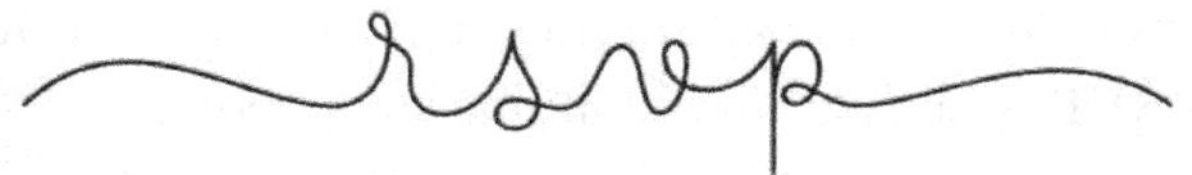

RSVP, or Répondez s'il vous plaît, is a French phrase meaning "please respond," and you better. Responding is crucial in the world of invitations. It's more than a formality; it's a respectful acknowledgment of the invitation and a commitment to attend or decline.

RSVP'ing promptly allows the host to finalize arrangements such as seating, catering, and other logistics. It demonstrates courtesy and consideration, ensuring the event runs smoothly and all guests are comfortably accommodated. By honoring invitations with a thoughtful RSVP, we contribute to the success of events, foster positive relationships, and uphold the values of respect and courtesy in our social interactions.

Respond promptly. Intentionally RSVP as soon as possible, ideally within a few days of receiving the invitation. This shows eagerness and respect for the host's timeline.

Be clear and polite. Clearly indicate whether you will attend, politely decline if you cannot, or explain any uncertainties. Use the method of RSVP specified on the invitation - phone, email, online form or other method when you respond.

Communicate graciously. If plans change after RSVPing, inform the host promptly. This allows them to adjust arrangements as well.

Plan your gift. Do not ever, EVER, attend an event without bringing a hostess gift or sending one in advance. It shows your gratitude and keeps you memorable in the eyes of her team. So, the next time you receive an invitation, embrace the joy it brings and respond with gratitude and consideration—it's the first step toward a memorable occasion, and cements the relationship for years to come.

A Capsule Wardrobe

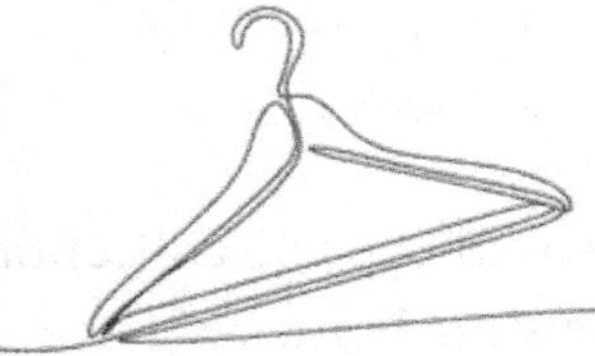

In the realm of refined personal presentation, a curated capsule collection becomes an anchor in etiquette, and the cornerstone of sophistication and style. The essence of a capsule collection lies in its ability to streamline a wardrobe into a crafted selection of versatile, timeless pieces, each chosen for its quality and adaptability. This thoughtful approach to dressing not only simplifies daily decision-making but also ensures that you are always prepared for any occasion with grace and confidence. In a world where fashion trends come and go, maintaining a capsule collection allows the focus to shift from fast-fashion fads to a personal brand of style and substance.

A capsule collection stands as a testament to the art of dressing with intention and grace. Where each piece in your wardrobe is chosen not just for its individual appeal, but for its ability to work seamlessly with the others. That's the sauce – where each garment in your closet (sans seasonal pops of style) can be paired with another; somehow and in some way.

At the heart of a well-crafted capsule collection are versatile tops—the unsung heroes of everyday dressing. Own a classic white button-down shirt that can transition effortlessly from a business meeting to a casual dinner, and a neutral t-shirt or a stylish blouse that can provide a solid foundation for countless outfits. Layering pieces like a chic cardigan, or a lightweight sweater adds an extra dimension of adaptability, allowing you to modify your look with ease as the temperature changes or as the occasion demands.

Classic bottoms are equally essential, providing the foundation upon which all other elements of the wardrobe are built. Own an impeccably tailored pants in a neutral color—black, navy, or beige—that can take you from a formal event to a semi-casual gathering. Alongside these, add a pair of dark-wash jeans for a casual yet refined alternative, perfect for less formal occasions. Owning a versatile skirt, whether it's a sleek pencil or a flowing A-line, ensures you have stylish options for a variety of settings.

Statement outerwear elevates the collection, transforming any outfit with a touch of sophistication. A tailored blazer in a classic color can add an air of professionalism to even the simplest ensemble, or a timeless trench coat that provides both style and function during cooler months. Outerwear is not merely functional, it's an integral part of a well-considered wardrobe that respects the balance between elegance and practicality.

Footwear in a capsule collection should strike a balance between style and comfort. You can't lose owning a pair of dress shoes or loafers in a neutral tone, ideal for both business and social occasions; and a pair of stylish, clean sneakers or ballet flats that cater to more relaxed settings. These choices reflect a commitment to your personal brand with thoughtfulness and dignity. Knowing these steps, literally, will walk you into the right rooms, at the right time, to get you in front of the right people.

Accessories play a subtle but significant role to your look by adding finishing touches that enhance your overall appearance. A purse, or versatile bag, perhaps a leather tote or a sleek crossbody, is both functional and chic, capable of holding your essentials while complementing any outfit. Simple yet elegant jewelry, such as diamonds or stud earrings, a classic watch, and a delicate necklace, adds a refined touch without being gaudy or overwhelming your look.

Seasonal adaptations will complete your look. Depending upon the time of year, include items like ear muffs and gloves for winter, a stylish scarf for the spring or fall, and sunglasses for summer. These additions ensure your wardrobe is prepared for all weather conditions, and demonstrates an unspoken understanding of appropriate dress for varying circumstances. A capsule collection is more than a strategic wardrobe choice; it embodies the principles of etiquette by emphasizing thoughtfulness, care, efficiency, and elegance. By carefully selecting pieces that work harmoniously together, you create a buildable wardrobe that is versatile and sophisticated. This minimizes clutter and decision fatigue, allowing you to dress with ease and confidence. It reflects an appreciation for quality over quantity and a respect for the nuances of different social and professional settings.

Maintaining a cohesive wardrobe through a capsule collection establishes a consistent personal style. This consistency in personal presentation conveys reliability and confidence, which are key aspects of good etiquette, more opportunities and increased wealth.

Fragrance Etiquette

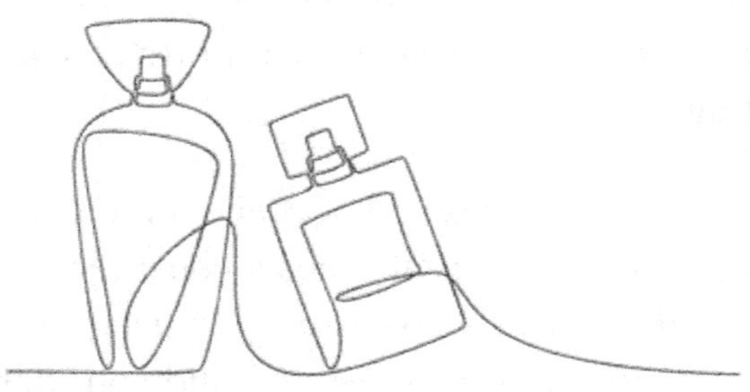

The connection between our sense of smell and our emotions is a powerful one. Research shows how aromas and fragrances influence how we feel, and how others feel about us. Finding the ideal scent isn't about buying expensive, on-trend fragrances, it's about indulging in a personal sensual experience. The right scent reveals so much about who you are, what you stand for, how you see yourself and what your presence means when you walk into a room.

How to pick the right scent. There are four fragrance families, with each having a place on the fragrance wheel invented by Michael Edwards; a world-renowned scent expert. The wheel is designed to help the fragrance industry standardize the development of scents, while offering buyers an organized way shop for scents that match their lifestyle.

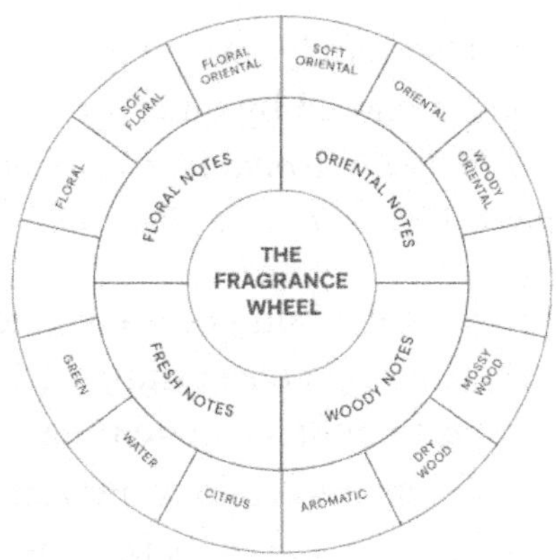

Floral. The floral scent family is described as a garden of fresh cut flowers. It is typically associated with women's fragrances, but can be infused into men's fragrances as well.
Subfamilies: Fruity, Floral, Soft Floral
Notes: Rose, Jasmine, Orange Blossom

Amber. This scent was previously known as oriental. This scent is described as "sensual," warm and "exotic."
Subfamilies: Soft Amber, Woody Amber
Notes: Vanilla, Myrrh, Anise

Woody. This family includes warm and opulent scents, mixing sandalwood and other incense-like fragrances like with drier notes like cedar.

Subfamilies: Woods, Mossy and Dry Woods
Notes: Patchouli, Vetiver, Sandalwood

Fresh. The fresh family has zingy, aromatic compositions anchored by quiet woodsy notes.
Subfamilies Include: Aromatic, Citrus, Water
Notes: Citrus, White Flowers, Bergamot

Beyond the aromatic body of scents, lies its strength. The varying concentrations, from potent parfums to lighter eau de toilettes, alters moods and affects impressions. Perfume strength directly influences its intensity and longevity on the skin.

Parfum, also known as perfume, perfume extract or extrait de parfum, has the highest concentration of aromatic compounds.
It typically contains 20% up to 40% perfume oils, and offers the longest-lasting fragrance experience, often lasting 6-8 hours or more on the skin. Sparingly apply this concentration, as it is quite expensive, and, due to its potency, is usually dabbed only on pulse points.

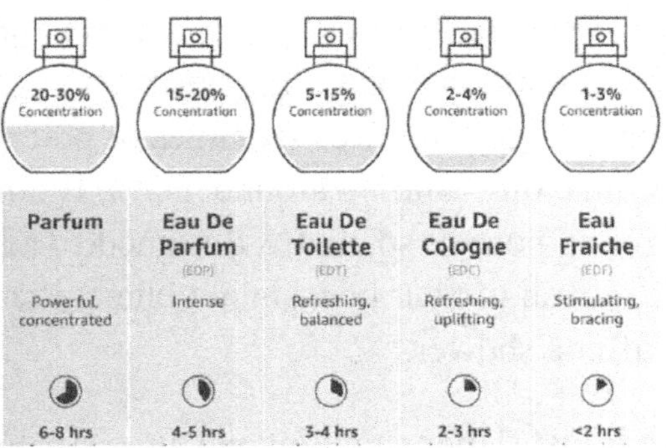

Eau de Parfum (EdP) is a better priced choice, and is known for its strong and long-lasting scent. It contains 15-20% perfume oils, and lasts around 4-5 hours on average. This strength is suitable for day or evening wear, and is usually applied to pulse points like wrists and neck.

Eau de Toilette (EdT) is lighter and more refreshing compared to EdP. It contains 5-15% perfume oils, and generally lasts 3-4 hours. This potency can be used liberally and is ideal for daily wear and warmer weather.

Eau de Cologne (EdC) is known for its lightness compared to more intense perfumes. It contains 2-4% perfume oils, and typically lasts 2-3 hours. Eau de cologne is used as a quick splash and suitable for casual or daytime use.

Eau de Fraîche (EdF) is the lightest in depth and concentration among fragrances and contains one of the lowest volumes of potency of perfume oils, landing around 1-3%. It only lasts for an hour or so, and is designed to add a quick refresh to your body in hot climates and right after a shower.

Make it last. Understanding perfume strengths helps you choose the right concentration for your body and lifestyle. Whichever scent and concentration you decide on, use a matching body wash, lotion, or oil before applying to create base that will help the scent last longer.

Storing your scents. Store your perfume away from direct sunlight; exposure to heat can cause the scent to break down and become less potent over time. Keep your bottles in a cool, dry area, to keep it fresh the last drop.

Try different scents until you feel comfortable showing up as your most authentic self.

Tools of the Table

Utensils are more than mere tools for eating—they are the instruments of etiquette, culture, and refinement that enhance our dining experiences. Whether dining casually, attending a formal banquet, or exploring international cuisines, understanding how to maneuver each piece with finesse is important. Knowing which utensil to use, and when, elevates your presence at the table and cements your presence among great company. From the precise placement of forks and knives to the subtle cues conveyed through their use, every gesture at the table speaks volumes about your respect for tradition and consideration of others.

The practicality of each piece plays a role during the discoveries of each course. Mastering utensil usage honors the timeless traditions that connect us through the universal language of food and hospitality. Each swipe of the napkin becomes a brushstroke in the art of dining etiquette.

Speaking of the napkin...the napkin on a table is a clear representation of the tone, atmosphere, dynamics, and emotions of the forthcoming dining experience. The fabrication, encasement and color of the napkin is the prologue to the story that is yet to come.

Entrée fork. The entrée fork, also known as the main fork or dinner fork, is the largest fork at a place setting. It features broader, longer and sturdier tines, and is used for cutting and spearing portions of meat, vegetables, and other main course items.

Salad fork. The salad fork is designed for enjoying salads or appetizers served before the main course in a formal dining setting. It is smaller than the dinner fork, and is placed to the left of the dinner fork – with both being placed to the left of the plate.

Fish fork. Fish forks are smaller and narrower than the dinner fork. Their slightly curved tines are designed to navigate seafood and delicate fish without damaging it.

Oyster, seafood or cocktail fork. Oyster forks are smaller and narrower than the fish fork. It's three or four short tines are very helpful when pulling delicacies from a shell.

Dessert fork. Dessert forks are one of the smallest on the table, and are used for desserts and fruit courses. They are placed horizontally above the dinner plate and just below the dessert spoon. Based upon the menu and formality of the meal, you may see only one of these, both, or neither one.

Butter knife. The wide, flat blade of the butter knife eases the spreading of butter or other soft toppings, covering a larger surface area with each stroke.

Dinner knife. The dinner knife is the partner to the entrée fork. These two pieces – along with a plate, napkin and water glass – will be in every table setting from a fast-casual diner to the finest continental setting.

Fish knife. Typically, narrower and sometimes slightly curved, this knife is designed for grip and comfort suitable for precision and control while cutting proper portions.

Steak knife. This utensil is serrated, and will be offered when steak or other meats that require cutting are served.

Dessert spoon. The dessert spoon has a slightly curved bowl, which allows for scooping and savoring a variety of desserts. From delicate mousses to creamy custards, its size is perfectly suited for portion control, offering a balance between function and elegance.

Coffee spoon. The coffee spoon is slightly shallower than a teaspoon, which makes it well-suited for stirring coffee and espresso. Its compact size allows for precise stirring without overwhelming smaller cups and glasses.

Teaspoon. This versatile utensil is able to handle small amounts of food and liquid; its role in stirring, measuring, and serving, makes it a valuable tool in casual, formal and everyday dining.

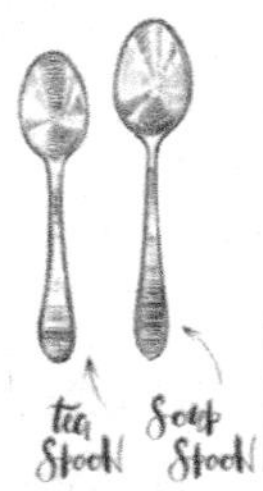

Soup spoon. Rounded and deeper than a regular spoon, this spoon used for consuming soups or broths.

The proper use of the most commonly used utensils is a reflection of your sophistication and appreciation of elevated standards.

Each Served Separately

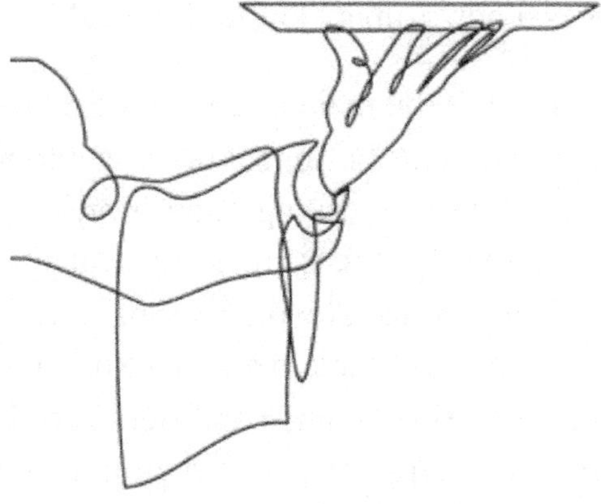

As we gather around the table for a meal, whether it's a simple family dinner or an elaborate formal affair, the structure and sequence of courses play a key role in defining the dining experience. Understanding these courses not only enhances our appreciation for culinary expression, but also guides us in navigating the social intricacies of dining etiquette.

At its heart, a meal is not merely sustenance but a shared journey of flavors and conversations. Each course serves a purpose, crafted to harmonize tastes, textures, and cultural influences. From the appetizers that awaken our palate and the comforting warmth of soups, to the refreshing crunch of salads, every course introduces a new dimension to the meal.

Moving through the main course, where hearty meats, delicate seafood, or savory vegetarian dishes take the stage, dining courses are designed to explore the richness of culinary diversity in all forms. Accompanying side dishes and sauces complement these main attractions, offering balance and depth to the dining moment. Desserts, with their decadent sweetness or refreshing lightness, provide a satisfying conclusion, leaving a lingering taste of indulgence. Each course contributes to the art of dining, and culinary craftsmanship.

In casual American dining, a typical meal often includes a starter such as soup or salad, a hearty main course like a burger or steak, and a simple dessert like pie or ice cream, offering a straight forward yet satisfying approach to eating.
3 courses: Appetizer, main course, and dessert.

4 courses: Hors d'oeuvre, appetizer, main course, and dessert.

In semi-formal dining, the meal typically comprises an appetizer or starter, a well-balanced main course with complementary sides, and a refined dessert. Offering a blend of casual comfort and elegant presentation.
5 courses: Hors d'oeuvre, appetizer, salad, main course, and dessert.
6 courses: Hors d'oeuvre, soup, appetizer, salad, main course, and dessert.
7 courses: Hors d'oeuvre, soup, appetizer, salad, main course, dessert, and mignardise.

In formal dining, the meal is elegantly structured with multiple courses, including an amuse-bouche, appetizer, soup, fish course, entrée, palate cleanser, cheese course, dessert, and coffee or petit fours, with each course meticulously crafted to provide a sophisticated and harmonious dining experience.
8 course meal: Hors d'oeuvre, soup, appetizer, salad, main course, palate cleanser, dessert, and mignardise.
9 course meal: Hors d'oeuvre, soup, appetizer, salad, fish, main course, palate cleanser, dessert, and mignardise.

A meal of ten or more courses always unfolds in unmatched precision. Beginning with an array of lavish amuse-bouches and appetizers, followed by a succession of refined courses including soups, fish, meats, palate cleansers, and elaborate desserts served in the most opulent manner.

10 course meal: Hors d'oeuvre, soup, appetizer, salad, fish, main course, palate cleanser, second main course, dessert, and mignardise.

12 course meal: Hors d'oeuvre, amuse-bouche, soup, appetizer, salad, fish, first main course, palate cleanser, second main course, cheese course, dessert, and mignardise.

From the simplicity of an American three-course meal to the elaborate sophistication of a Black tie twelve-course feast, each course explores traditional and innovative elements, offering insights into how they come together to form a cohesive culinary journey.

Continental Dining

The world of Continental dining, is steeped in tradition, history, elegance, and a dash of European flair. The story of Continental dining begins in the grand estates of Europe centuries ago. It was here that elaborate feasts and banquets were hosted, showcasing not only the wealth of the hosts but also their sophistication in matters of dining etiquette. From the courts of Louis XIV in Versailles to the salons of Vienna and the grand dining rooms of London and Rome, Continental dining evolved as a symbol of refinement, cultural prowess, and influence.

In the 18th and 19th centuries, Continental Dining etiquette became codified into a set of rules and traditions that governed how one should present themselves at the table. These rules were not merely about manners; they were a reflection of social status, education, and respect for culinary arts. The use of multiple utensils, the order of service, and even the seating arrangements—all played a part in signaling were you "sat" in society.

The chef is the star. Central to Continental dining is its exquisite cuisine. French, Italian, Austrian, and other European culinary traditions melded together to create a tapestry of flavors and techniques that was original and captivating. From delicate French sauces to hearty Italian pastas and Austrian pastries, Continental cuisine celebrates diversity while adhering to principles of balance, quality ingredients, and preparation.

Each dish tells a story of its region, its history, and the artisans who perfected it over time and generations. Whether it's coq au vin (a French chicken stew) simmered to perfection, a tender wiener schnitzel (thinly sliced veal that's cooked coated with breadcrumbs and no sauce) with a crispy golden crust, or a velvety tiramisu (an Italian dessert made of ladyfinger pastries dipped in coffee, layered with a whipped mixture of eggs, sugar and mascarpone that's flavored with cocoa) that melts in your mouth, continental dining promises a sensory journey that delights the palate and nourishes the soul.

Elegance meets precision. Every little detail matters, from the placement of the napkin to the arrangement of the silverware. The table setting itself is a work of intentional art, meticulously designed to enhance the experience and showcase the beauty of the meal.

More than manners. Beyond the culinary delights and impeccable table settings, Continental dining is about etiquette—a code of conduct that reflects cultural norms and values. It's about respecting the chef's artistry, and engaging in meaningful conversation with fellow diners.

Etiquette dictates everything from how to hold a wine glass (by the stem, never the bowl) to when to use a bread roll to mop up sauce (only discreetly). It's a dance of gestures and signals, where a raised eyebrow can signal admiration for a dish and a subtle nod acknowledges the host's hospitality.

The fanfare of the food. In today's world, continental dining has adapted to embrace new culinary trends and global influences while preserving its core principles of elegance and respect. Chefs experiment with fusion cuisines, blending traditional recipes with contemporary twists to create dishes that surprise and delight. Restaurants around the globe offer dining experiences that cater to diverse palates, ensuring that everyone—from the seasoned connoisseur to the curious novice—can partake in this timeless tradition. Whether you're dining in a Michelin-starred restaurant in Paris, a cozy trattoria in Florence, or a chic bistro in New York City, the essence of this style remains. It's about a celebration of good food, good company, and the joy of shared experiences.

The Language of Cutlery

In the quiet elegance of a well-appointed dining room, cutlery becomes more than mere tools for eating—it becomes a language, speaking volumes about tradition, sophistication, and the art of dining itself. From the delicate balance of a salad fork to the sturdy grace of a steak knife, each utensil tells a story, weaving together threads of culture, history, and culinary mastery.

Start. When you sit down for a meal and pick up your fork and knife, that's the start of the cutlery language. Your utensils are ready to help you enjoy the food that's coming your way. They're your partners for the meal, helping you get excited about what's on your plate.

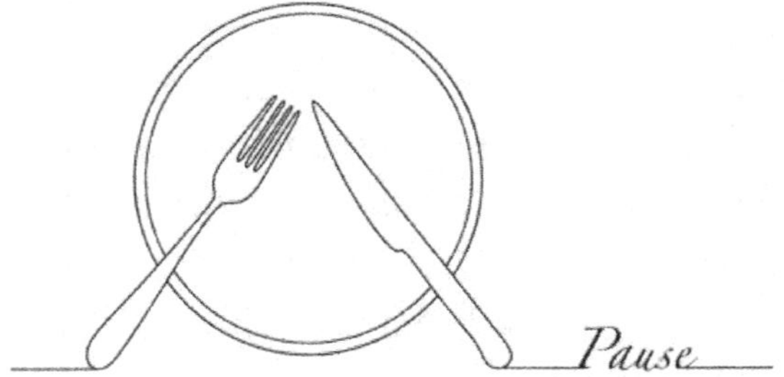

Pause. Placing your fork at an angle with the tines facing up, and your knife in an opposing angle (blade in) signals to the server that you're taking a break, and taking a moment to slow down and savor the moment.

Excellent. Positioning your utensils facing the right signals your server to send compliments to the kitchen; that your meal was cooked well and tasted great.

Did not like. Placing your knife through the lower tine of your fork sends out a glaring signal that you did not like nor enjoy your meal, and you don't want to finish it. It is okay to not love everything you try; but, let your utensils do the talking for you.

Next dish: After you finish one plate of food, and are ready for more place your knife facing left, blade downy and position your fork on top of the knife with the tines pointing towards 12 noon on a clock.

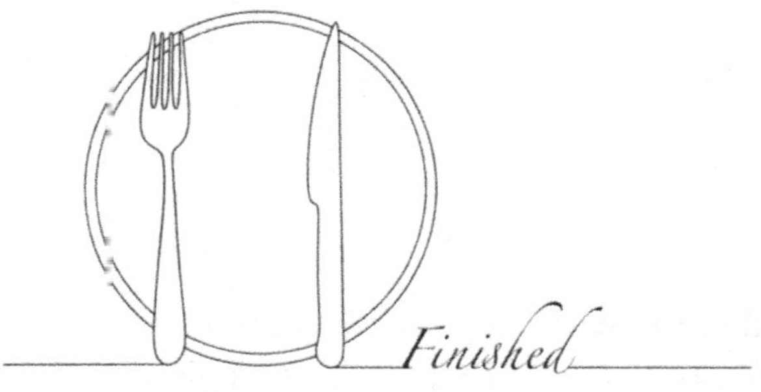

Finished: When you've had your fill and your fork and knife are resting neatly on your plate, is shows that you've enjoyed your meal and you're satisfied. Your utensils are saying, "Job well done!"

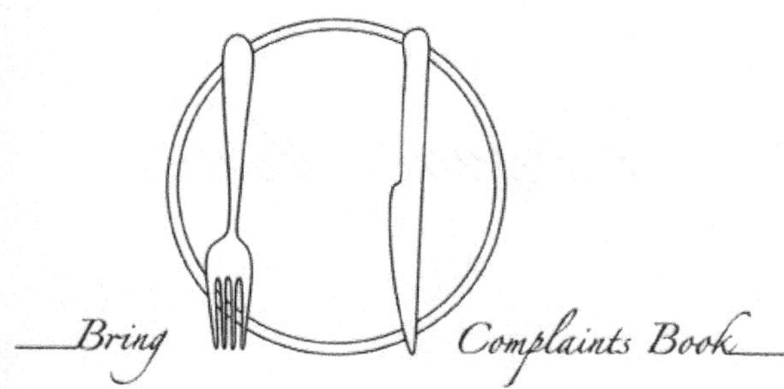

Bring complaints book. If something isn't quite right with your meal let your fork and knife signal for the complaints book. You're saying, "Hi, we need to talk about this." Once your server sees your utensils in this position you will be addressed rather quickly so as not to create a commotion. Speak quietly, politely and in a reserved tone.

Try not to embarrass the server, the Maître d', the chef or anyone else. Remember, people are always watching, handle the situation with grace and tact. Once someone comes over to address your concern, have in mind whether you want the meal recooked or if you would like to order something else – speak with intention and have a resolution in mind.

From the sparkling clarity of a champagne flute to the intricate design of a brandy snifter, the variety of glasses used in formal settings serves both practical and aesthetic functions, reflecting the importance of etiquette in every aspect of casual and social interactions.

Water glass. The water glass, larger than other glasses, is used for serving water throughout the meal. Its size accommodates refills and ensures guests have a sufficient supply of water. A little ice is okay in the glass, but too much may cause a distraction at the table as it clinks around in the glass.

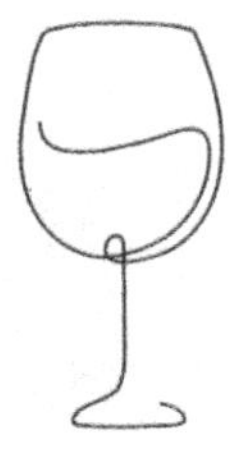

Red wine glass. This glass is designed to enhance the flavor and aroma of red wines. They have a wide bowl with a narrow rim to allow the wine to breathe and release its essence.

White wine glass. White wine glasses are smaller than their red counterpart. They are designed to preserver the cooler temperature of white wines as indicated by its tapered rim.

Champagne flute. Champagne and sparkling wines are served in a flute glass. The tall, narrow shape reduces the amount of oxygen that can get into the glass. This feature helps retain the aroma and the champagne's carbonation.

Port glass. Port glasses, known for serving dessert wines, have a rounded bowl to allow for the wine's flavors to be appreciated. The shape of the glass – very rounded then narrow at the top – helps to concentrate the aromas allowing for a more intense sensory experience.

Martini glass. The classic martini glass design and function play a significant role in formal dining and cocktail etiquette with its cone-shape, wide rim and stem. Cocktails other than a martini can be served in this glass as well. Beverages served in martini glasses are often garnished with olives, lemon twists, or cherries. Garnish adds visual appeal and complements the cocktail's flavor profile.

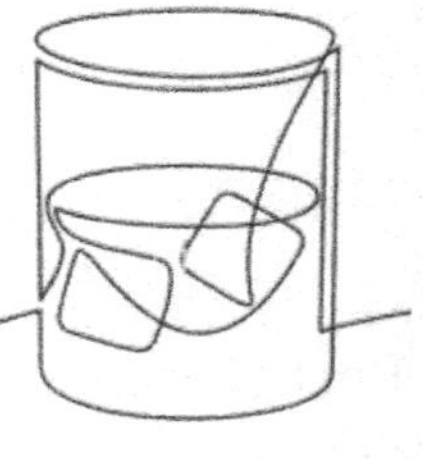

Old Fashioned, Rocks or Low-Ball glass: This is used for serving cocktails that are typically served over ice. It's made with a thick, sturdy base to provide stability and a solid feel in hand.

Irish coffee glass. This glass serves beverages that combine coffee with alcohol. Its shape enhances the presentation of the beverage, while the handle supports the functionality aspect of serving hot beverages.

Brandy snifters. Brandy snifters are used for serving brandy and aromatic spirits. The wide bowl allows for the spirit to be warmed by hand and the narrow rim concentrates the aromas.

The careful selection and use of appropriate glasses for beverages are essential to both the enjoyment and the etiquette of fine drinking. Let the glass you use not only reflect your personal style but also honor the traditions that elevate every sip into a moment of sophisticated indulgence.

This Calls for a Toast

Nothing marks a significant moment with eloquence and sincerity more than a toast. The raising of a glass that publicly blends a heartfelt message with this time-honored ceremonial gesture. At some point in your adult life you will be asked to give a toast, or you may suddenly realize in the middle of a special event that "This calls for a toast!" Don't worry about being perfectly eloquent, let your authenticity in the moment be what matters the most. Whether the toast is planned – say for a special party, wedding, graduation, anniversary gala or other celebratory event – or its impromptu, here is a quick formula for making a perfect toast every time.

Start with a Greeting

Address the audience or the guest(s) of honor. "Ladies and gentlemen," or "Dear friends,"

State the Occasion

Clearly mention the event or reason for the toast. "We are here to celebrate [occasion]," or "Today marks a special milestone."

Share a Personal Touch

Include a brief, meaningful sentiment or anecdote related to the occasion or the person being honored. This could be a compliment, a memory, or a wish.

Offer Your Toast

Make your main point and extend your wishes. "Here's to [the person/occasion]—may [wish or positive sentiment]."

Raise Your Glass

Conclude by inviting everyone to join you in raising their glasses and offering a collective "Cheers" or a similar expression of celebration.

The toast should last two to five minutes. Anything longer can disrupt the flow of the evening's events.

Eating Difficult Foods

Eating difficult foods can pose a challenge, especially in formal settings where grace and propriety are important. Whether they're challenging due to the preparation, taste, or cultural unfamiliarity, this moment during the meal requires finesse and tact to navigate gracefully to the next course. From shellfish like shrimp and lobster to escargot and foods that might not align with your personal taste preferences, there are ways to handle such situations without offending your host or fellow diners.

Crustaceans. In most dining settings you will be provided with a shell cracker and seafood fork. Start with the claws. Gently take one claw in your hand and use the cracker to break open the hard shell. Apply firm but controlled pressure to crack the shell without crushing the meat inside. Once the shell is cracked, carefully extract the meat using a seafood fork. The meat of the claw should come out in large chunks. Repeat this process with the other claw.

A shellfish like lobster will arrive with the tail already split open. Gently pry the shell apart to reveal the tender flesh inside. Use a seafood fork to pull the meat up and out in one piece. Don't forget to explore the small, hidden pockets of meat found in the lobster's legs and underbelly. Use a seafood fork or small pick, to extract any remaining meat from these areas. If your lobster is served with drawn butter dip each piece of meat into the melted butter, and eat it with your fork. Eating lobster celebrates both the bounty of the sea and the art of dining.

Escargot. The sight of this classic French appetizer might seem strange at first, but if it's presented to you and it's not appealing – take at least one bite. Begin by holding the escargot shell with the escargot tongs (which will be brough with the dish). Gently grip the shell to steady it without applying too much pressure. Use the snail fork in your opposite hand to carefully extract the escargot from its shell. It should extract smoothly as this delicacy is typically served in a bath of garlic butter.

Use designated utensils, such as snail tongs and forks, to extract escargot from shells gracefully. If you're still unsure about consuming a particular dish, observe others and follow their lead in terms of technique and pace.

Spaghetti. If your spaghetti is served with a rich, thick sauce, it's often a good idea to use the fork to twirl the pasta. A spoon might be used in some cultures or formal settings, but the fork alone is generally acceptable. Hold the fork with your dominant hand. Start by placing the tines of the fork into the spaghetti and twirl the fork gently to gather a small portion of pasta. Avoid taking too much at once to not look greedy and to keep your place setting and outfit sauce-free.

Twirl the pasta against the edge of the plate or bowl to help it coil neatly around the fork. In most settings, using a spoon to assist with twirling the pasta isn't necessary. However, if a spoon is provided and you feel it is more comfortable, you may use it discreetly. Take small, manageable bites. If there's excess sauce on the plate, do not use your fork to scoop it up. Instead, use the edge of the fork to gather small amounts of sauce with the pasta. If the sauce drips, use your napkin to gently dab the area. Do not use your napkin to wipe your mouth or hands excessively. Remember to keep it classy, there is more to the dinner than the meal.

Removing unwanted food from your mouth. As you elevate you will come across foods, among other things, that you're not familiar with. That's supposed to happen. When you're presented a food with a challenging texture or taste, take small bites to gauge your reaction. If you absolutely cannot swallow the bite, discreetly remove it from your mouth with a fork and hide it under another food item close to the edge of your plate. Do not criticize the taste and avoid direct negativity or refusal; instead, focus on the overall dining experience and conversations.

At Your Service

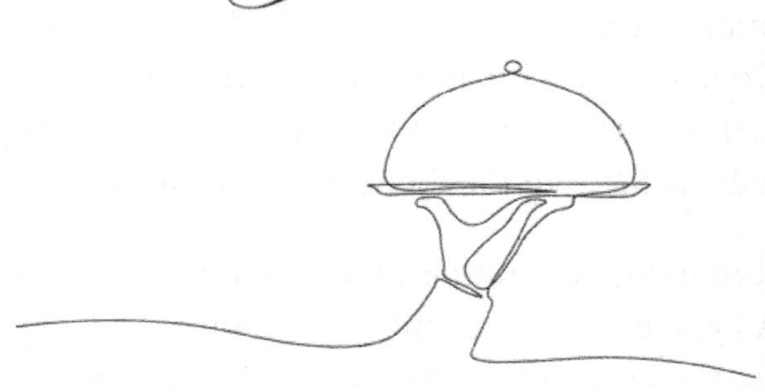

In the elegant ambiance of a formal dining establishment, the role of waitstaff is both crucial and intricate, embodying the essence of refined service and attention to detail. The expectations placed on these professionals are high, as they are the primary facilitators of a seamless and memorable dining experience. Each action, from the initial greeting to the final farewell, reflects a commitment to excellence.

Throughout the dining experience, waitstaff must maintain an unobtrusive yet attentive presence. They are responsible for monitoring the guests' needs without interrupting their conversation or enjoyment.

Responsibilities include

Menu presentation

Menu navigation

Ingredient knowledge

Potential allergens

Accurate order taking (noting special requests)

Coordination with the kitchen

Beverage recommendations

Managing guest complaints

Clearing the table after each course

Check presentation with explanation of charges

Processing payments (if applicable)

Expectation of a polished appearance

A good demeanor

The waitstaff are servers, not servants. Their role is to provide exemplary service to ensure a memorable dining experience for all guests, not just you.

Serving staff should be tipped 15% to 25%, if applicable.

American Dining

Before fast food and food trucks ruled the land, American dining was all about hearty meals cooked over an open fire. Early settlers huddled around a campfire, roasting up game meat, cornbread, and beans— simple and satisfying nourishment to fuel their adventures. As settlers spread across America's landscape, regional flavors started to pop up. In the South, soulful dishes like fried chicken and collard greens were popularized. Out West, cowboys rustled up chili and hearty stews. And up North, seafood chowder warmed the bellies of sailors and fishermen braving the cold seas.

Fast forward to the 19th and 20th centuries, and America became a melting pot of cultures—and cuisines. Immigrants from around the world brought their own flavors and culinary traditions, adding spice (literally!) to the American dining scene.

Italian immigrants introduced us to mouthwatering pizzas and pasta dishes that quickly became household favorites. Chinese immigrants brought the bold flavors of stir-fries and dim sum, while Mexican cuisine brought us tacos, burritos, and guacamole galore.

Enslaved Africans from regions like Senegal, Gambia, and Sierra Leone, brought extensive knowledge of rice cultivation. They played a major role in establishing rice plantations in the Carolinas and Georgia, making rice a staple crop in Southern cuisine.

Retro diners to hipster hangouts. The 20th century saw American dining evolve in exciting ways. The rise of diners in the 1950s became iconic, with jukeboxes, milkshakes, and burgers becoming symbols of American culture. In the swinging '60s and '70s, America embraced casual dining with a side of disco fever. Think TV dinners (complete with aluminum trays), and the birth of fast-food restaurants. It was all about convenience without sacrificing flavor, hence the prevalence of drive-thru's.

American dining is now upscaled and artisanal. Hipster cafes brew small-batch coffee while farm-to-table restaurants serve up seasonal dishes sourced locally. Food trucks roam the streets offering gourmet tacos, fusion cuisine, and Instagram-worthy treats that blend flavors from around the globe. Social media has turned food into art, with hashtags and food bloggers documenting every delicious bite.

So, what's your signature flavor of American dining? Your personal brand requires that. Whether you're digging into classic comfort food, trying a trendy fusion dish, or savoring a farm-fresh meal, your personal brand should reflect a celebration of diversity, creativity, and taste. And your table manners must demonstrate your comfort – no matter how uncomfortable – with all types of foods and meal settings.

Table Manners

In the elegant realm of formal dining, each plate, utensil and glass are meticulously placed upon the table to serve a purpose, guiding your dining experience through a symphony of flavors and textures among friends, school mates, family and colleagues. The gleam of polished silverware catches the soft glow of candle light, adding a touch of refinement to the arranged table. Each piece isn't just there; it's placed with thoughtfulness, adding to the overall charm of the evening. And those glasses? They sparkle like they know they're holding something special—maybe a fine wine or some flavored fancy water to keep you hydrated between bites. It sets a stage where each course is not just nourishment but an artful presentation, where every detail speaks to the care and consideration of the evening. In this setting, the utensils become more than tools—they are instruments of elegance, guiding guests through a memorable evening of sophisticated dining.

Arrival. You should arrive 15-30 minutes before the scheduled start of the event to get to know the other dinner guests, enjoy a welcome drink, and settle in.

Cocktail hour. An open bar during the cocktail hour at formal events, such as weddings, galas, and corporate functions is quite common. It offers guests an opportunity to mingle, enjoy a cocktail, and get comfortable before the main festivities. An open bar means that guests can order drinks without paying for them; that doesn't mean, "keep drinking because the drinks are free." The drinks aren't actually free – the host is paying for them on behalf of each guest. Although the drinks are free, cap your drinks at two. People are watching and you don't want to get too loose and possibly lose opportunities before the evening gets started. If the bartender has a tip cup out you should tip, even during an open bar.

Hors d'oeuvres. Hors d'oeuvres are small, often elegant dishes served before a meal. They are an essential part of many formal and informal dining events. If hors d'oeuvres are being passed by servers, wait until a server approaches you with the tray. If the hors d'oeuvres are set up on a table or buffet, use the tongs, forks, or spoons that should be placed nearby. When serving yourself from a platter or tray, take one piece of each type of hors d'oeuvre at a time, rather than taking multiple pieces at once. If the hors d'oeuvres are designed to be eaten with your fingers, hold them delicately and take small bites. While it's tempting to sample many items, take it easy so you have room for the next round of appetizers, the main courses and desserts. As the cocktail hour or hors d'oeuvres service comes to an end, finish your current hors d'oeuvre or set aside your plate and drink before moving to the next course or area. The waitstaff will likely circle back to collect your items as you transition to the main dining area.

Approaching the table: Approach the dining table calmly and gracefully. Wait for the host or hostess to indicate where you should sit, or if seating yourself, choose a place where you feel comfortable.

Napkin placement and unfolding. As soon as you're seated, unfold your napkin and place it neatly on your lap – never tuck it in your shirt. In formal settings, wait for your host or the lead guest to take up their napkin before you do.

Napkin uses during the meal. Use your napkin to gently dab or blot your mouth as needed during the meal. Avoid wiping your mouth back and forth, you'll look messy, rude or overly casual. Your napkin should never be used to clean utensils or other items. If your utensils have spots, or don't look clean, simply (and quietly) ask your server to replace them.

If your napkins drops. If your napkin falls to the floor during the meal, politely ask for a replacement from the staff.

Review the utensils. Take a moment to familiarize yourself with the utensils on the table and their arrangement. This will give an indication on the number of courses being served and what those courses may include.

Watch the room. Remain seated and wait for a signal from the host or master of ceremonies indicating that it is time to begin. This could be the host making a welcome speech, a toast, or a simple indication that the meal has started. Do not start eating or drinking until you receive this cue.

F.O.R.D. Once the dinner formally begins take time to get to know your table mates. Use this time to get to know new people, or strengthen existing relationships. If you're not sure what to say to get the conversation, use the F.O.R.D. method. This stands for family, occupation, recreation and dreams. I would also add in P. for pets. These are very safe topics for conversation over dinner. Try and stay away from politics and religion. Even if you're attending a political event, talk about the people in politics but not your specific political beliefs. Here are a few conversation starters:

Family ~ *"I'm curious, do you have any family traditions that you have coming up?"* or *"Do you have family in the area?"*

Occupation ~ *"I noticed you mentioned you work in [specific field/industry], how did you get started in that field?"* or *"What do you do?"* or *"What do you do for work?"*

Recreation ~ *"What do you have planned for this weekend?"* or *"What do you like to do for fun?"*

Dreams ~ *"What's something you'd like to try in the future?"* or *"So, what's your plan after retirement?"*

Pets ~ *"I'd love to hear about your pet. What kind do you have?"* or *"What's the funniest thing your pet has done?"*

Water. Enjoy a few sips of water at the start of the meal to cleanse your palate before you begin eating, between bites and courses. Keep it half full throughout the meal to ensure hydration and to aid in digestion.

Listen. Listen attentively to others when they speak, showing genuine interest in their stories and opinions. Avoid interrupting and wait for natural pauses to contribute to the conversation and share your views.

Include everyone. Make an effort to include all guests in the conversation, ensuring that no one feels left out or excluded from the discussion.

Personal space. Be mindful of the immediate area around you and others. Avoid leaning over other diners or speaking too loudly, especially in intimate settings.

Time to eat. For a formal or semi-formal dinner (Continental dining), utensils are laid out in the order they will be used, starting from the outside and moving inward toward the plate. Forks are placed on the left side of the plate, while knives and spoons are on the right. Start with the outermost utensils for the first course and progress inward with each subsequent course. It's a symphony of symmetry and sophistication, where even the smallest deviation from tradition can evoke a gasp from seasoned dining enthusiasts.

Wine during the meal. You will likely be offered the appropriate wine glass for each type of wine served. Hold the glass by the stem to avoid warming the wine with your hand. Sip wine slowly and in moderation, pairing it with each course as recommended by your host or sommelier.

Soup. Wait for the soup course to be served by the waitstaff or when it is announced as part of the meal. Do not start eating or reach for the soup until everyone at the table has been served and the host indicates that it's time to begin. Soups are eaten with a soup spoon, which is generally larger and rounder than a dessert spoon (see page 44). If the soup is too hot, allow it to cool slightly – do not blow it to cool the temperature. You can gently stir the soup with your spoon to help it cool evenly. When you're ready, dip your spoon into the bowl and scoop away from you (towards an imaginary 12 o'clock) then lift the spoon and bring it towards your mouth – you can lean in but do not lean over the bowl. If dining casually you can tilt the bowl away from you to scoop the last bit of soup in the bottom of the bowl. If you are dining formally, scoop what you can and leave the rest – do not try to scoop your soup bowl clean.

Salad. Since salads are mainly served at the top of a meal, do not begin eating until everyone at the table has been served and it is appropriate to start. Salad is typically eaten with a salad fork, which is smaller and placed to the left of the dinner plate. If the salad course is served with a main course, you may use the outermost fork. The salad may arrive dressed with additional dressing resting in a boat on the table. If you'd like more dressing on your salad ask a table mate to pass it to you, do not reach over anyone or anything to get it.

Bread: Tear off small pieces of bread with your fingers and butter each piece individually using the butter knife provided. Then raise to eat it. Keep the unbuttered bread on your bread plate.

Passing the bread basket. If the bread basket is passed around the table, take a piece and offer it to your neighbor to the right before taking one for yourself.

Eating your food. The entrée is served with specific utensils, which are often the main course fork and knife. These utensils are usually the ones closest to the plate or on the outer edges of the utensil setting.

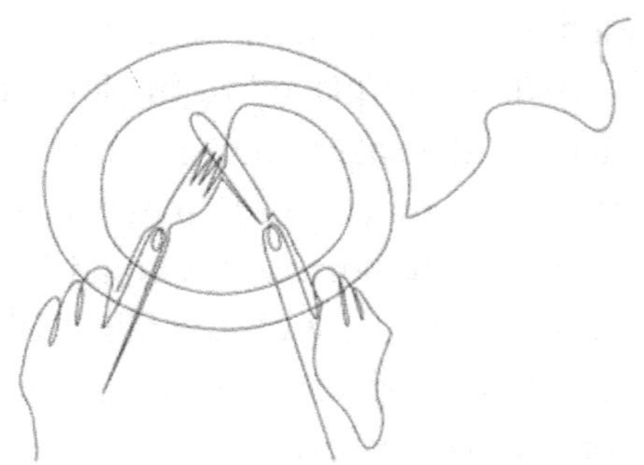

In Continental style dining (formal), the fork is held in the left hand with its times facing downward, hold the knife in your right hand. Use your index finger to apply the necessary pressure to cut your food and push each bite onto the fork. Only cut what you are about to eat. Food is cut into bite-sized pieces while still on the plate. The fork remains in the left hand, and is used to bring each bite to your mouth, tines down.

American style dining reflects a more casual and less formal approach to dining compared to Continental style. It allows for a more relaxed and practical method of eating. In American style dining, the fork is used in the left hand – tines down to hold the food in place; while the knife is used in the right hand for cutting the food. The fork is switched to the right hand as the bite is raised into your mouth.

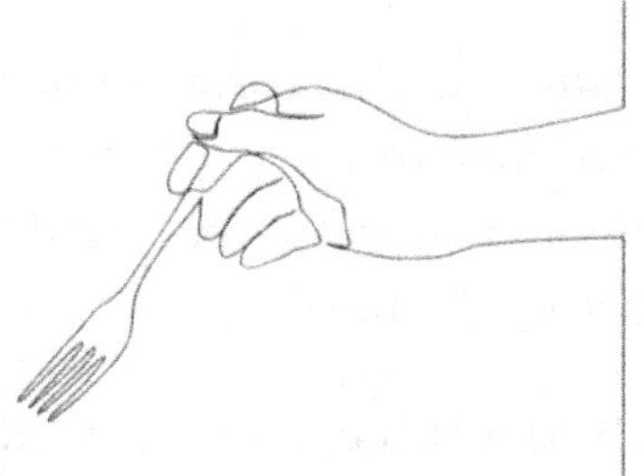

American style dining is more casual and food is constantly switching between your left and right hands.

Removing unwanted food from your mouth. See page 63

Keeping your hands clean. Use your napkin to dab your fingers lightly between bites, if necessary, especially when eating finger foods or foods that may leave residue on your hands.

Finger bowl. In some dining experiences you may use your hands and fingers instead of utensils. In these instances, your server will bring you a finger bowl at the end of the meal. These bowls are filled with water and often garnished with a slice of lemon or a few flower petals to add a touch of elegance. Rinse your fingers discreetly for a quick refresh before leaving the table.

Passing dishes: When passing condiments or dishes, offer them to your right-hand side to allow guests to take what they need without reaching across the table.

Eating fish. If a fish course is served, you may see a fish knife and fork at your setting. Use the fish fork to hold the fish steady while gently separating the flesh with the fish knife. Do so with a steady hand and avoid cutting into bones or causing unnecessary mess.

Blotting spills. If you accidentally spill something on yourself or the table, use your napkin to blot the spill immediately. Blotting rather than wiping helps to absorb the liquid without spreading it further.

Temporarily leaving the table. When temporarily leaving the table during the meal to hit the dance floor or head to the restroom, loosely fold your napkin and place it to the left of your plate. This signals to the waitstaff that you are not finished and intend to return.

Dessert. If dessert is served with utensils, such as cake or fruit, use the dessert fork and spoon provided. Hold the fork in your left hand and the spoon in your right hand. Take small bites and savor the flavors of the dessert.

Napkin placement after the meal: Once you have finished your meal, gently fold your napkin loosely and place it to the left of your plate. This signals to the server – in addition to the placement of your utensils (see page 56) – that you have finished dining.

Depart gracefully. Leave the dining area as you found it, push your chair in, and tidy up any personal belongings. Bid farewell to fellow guests with warmth and appreciation for their company. Get their contact information so you can follow up in 2 days, 2 weeks and 2 months.

Thank the hosts: Express gratitude to the hosts for their hospitality and for organizing the gathering. Offer to assist with clearing the table or cleaning up if dining at someone's home. You should have given them their hostess gift upon arrival but that is not always possible. Handing your gift to them before you leave is acceptable as well.

The Finishing Touch

Whether dining at home, in a restaurant, or at a formal event, embrace the opportunity to indulge in fine cuisine and cultural traditions. Enjoy the journey of exploring new flavors and enhancing your appreciation for culinary arts. The impact of manners and etiquette extends far beyond mere social niceties; they play a pivotal role in shaping your image and influencing earning potential. Personal branding plays a crucial role in career advancement and business success, the significance of manners and etiquette cannot be overstated.

Your ability to navigate conversations with grace, and handle social cues effectively sets you apart. People remember those who make them feel respected and valued, and this can translate into important connections, referrals, and opportunities. These connections often lead to higher-paying roles, lucrative contracts, or strategic partnerships that might otherwise remain out of reach.

As you apply these principles in your daily life, remember that etiquette is not a static set of rules but a dynamic practice that evolves with experiences and interactions. It is a lifelong journey of learning and adapting, where each encounter provides an opportunity to refine and express your understanding of respect and grace. From the correct use of utensils at a formal dinner to the subtle art of conversation at a networking event, each aspect of etiquette fosters understanding and connection among global citizens.

The dividends of good manners are worth more than any value of investment.

Saideh's Other Books

Bloodline: A Generational Wealth Playbook
2018

Editor, Successful Drug-Free Psychotherapy for Schizophrenia with Dr. Revella Levin
2018

Happiness in Heels
2017

Courage To Climb
2016

Don't Wait To Lose Weight
2014

Life Remixed
2012

100 Words of Wisdom for Women
2005

Plus four others

Made in United States
Orlando, FL
30 July 2024

49754385R00049